Little Learning Labs

KITCHEN SCIENCE FOR KIDS

26 Family-Friendly Experiments for Fun Around the House

QUARRY

LIZ LEE HEINECKE

DEDICATION:

TO CHARLIE, MAY, AND SARAH

Brimming with creative inspiration, how-to projects, and useful information to enrich your everyday life, Quarto Knows is a favorite destination for those pursuing their interests and passions. Visit our site and dig deeper with our books into your area of interest: Quarto Creates, Quarto Cooks, Quarto Homes, Quarto Lives, Quarto Drives, Quarto Explores, Quarto Gifts, or Quarto Kids.

© 2014 Quarto Publishing Group USA Inc.
Text © 2014 Amber Procaccini Photography

First Published in 2018 by Quarry Books, an imprint of The Quarto Group,
100 Cummings Center, Suite 265-D, Beverly, MA 01915, USA.
T (978) 282-9590 F (978) 283-2742 QuartoKnows.com

Quarry Books titles are also available at discount for retail, wholesale, promotional, and bulk purchase. For details, contact the Special Sales Manager by email at specialsales@quarto.com or by mail at The Quarto Group, Attn: Special Sales Manager, 401 Second Avenue North, Suite 310, Minneapolis, MN 55401, USA.

10 9 8 7 6 5 4 3 2 1

ISBN: 978-1-63159-562-2

Digital edition published in 2018
The content in this book originally appeared in the book *Kitchen Science Lab for Kids* (Quarry Books, 2014).

Design: Leigh Ring // www.ringartdesign.com
Photography: Amber Procaccini Photography // www.aprocacciniphoto.com

Printed in China

CONTENTS

INTRODUCTION

WHEN IT COMES TO INTRODUCING KIDS TO SCIENCE, THERE'S NO PLACE LIKE HOME.

The sparks of curiosity and creativity are first ignited in kitchens and backyards, and these are ideal venues for delving into the amazing world of science. Performing experiments in a familiar environment, without time limits or the pressure of grades, kids discover that science isn't hard or scary, and that they can find it everywhere they look. Best of all, there are a number of projects you can do with what you already have on hand.

When I was young, activities like playing Twenty Questions, collecting rocks, and catching frogs fueled my interest in the natural world, eventually leading me to study science and art. After ten years of bench work in research labs, I embarked on a new adventure: staying at home with three young children.

When my youngest was two, we added Science Wednesdays to the family calendar. Each week, the kids looked forward to trying a science project, taking a nature walk, or visiting a zoo or science museum. It was a fun way to change things up from the usual crayons and play dough.

Unfortunately, many of the experiments I found required specialized equipment, when the last thing I wanted to do was to drag three kids to the hardware store. Calling on my experience in research labs, I started customizing traditional science experiments, and making up a few new ones, with three goals in mind. The projects had to be safe enough for my youngest, engaging enough for my oldest, and would ideally use ingredients I already had around the house.

With our new collection of kitchen pantry experiments, we explored the amazing worlds of physics, chemistry, and biology together. My two-year-old would engage in the projects at the simplest level, often just playing with the ingredients, while my oldest would tackle the science with gusto to see what would happen.

Sunny days found us hunting caterpillars and making s'mores in pizza box solar ovens, while cold and rainy days were livened up by bubbling, color-changing concoctions. We did experiments with yeast and made pizza dough to see how microbiology is used in food preparation. Our backyard became a physics lab for throwing eggs and shooting marshmallows. Litmus paper collages and alum crystal geodes adorned the house as we found beautiful ways to combine science and art.

Our first science journals are now treasured keepsakes, filled with scribbles, illustrations, dates, and awkwardly penned words like "surface tension." The crayon drawings of butterflies, volcanoes, and tie-dye milk are priceless.

To this day, my kids come running when I suggest trying a new or favorite science experiment. I hope yours will too.

OVERVIEW

There's a treasure trove of science experiments hiding in your refrigerator, pantry, and junk drawer. This book will introduce you to fun, educational projects for your family to explore, using things you may already have on hand.

Each experiment contains an easy-to-understand explanation of the science behind the project to introduce you to the vocabulary and ideas you're exploring.
The labs are set up to make science as easy as following a recipe with sections detailing:

→ Materials
→ Safety Tips and Hints
→ Protocol (instructions)
→ The Science Behind the Fun
→ Creative Enrichment

The MATERIALS section lists all the ingredients you'll need to conduct each experiment. SAFETY TIPS AND HINTS will give you some common-sense guidelines for doing the experiments. PROTOCOL is a scientific word for instructions, and each protocol will take you step-by-step through the basics of the experiment. THE SCIENCE BEHIND THE FUN offers simple scientific explanations for each experiment and CREATIVE ENRICHMENT will give you variations or ideas for taking the project a step or two further. Hopefully, you'll be inspired to come up with some additional ideas of your own.

For kids, science is as much about the process as the results. Measuring, scooping, stirring, and messy hands are all part of the experience, and many of the safe chemical reactions in the book feel cold, are sticky, or have a distinct odor, allowing kids to use all of their senses as they immerse themselves in the experience. Some experiments can even morph into art projects for those who love visual creations. Most are simple to clean up.

My kids and I have tested all of these experiments, and they will work well if you follow the protocol closely. However, some may involve tweaking or practice for perfect results. Remember, mistakes and troubleshooting are far more educational than perfection, and in science, many laboratory blunders have led to great discoveries.

SCIENCE JOURNAL

Every scientist keeps a notebook to document and detail studies and experiments. The scientific method involves asking a question, making observations, and performing experiments that address the question.

If you want to make your own science journal, find a spiral notebook, composition book, or staple some blank pieces of paper together. Write your name on the cover and use your notebook to keep track of all the great experiments you do. Take your journal on nature walks or vacations and use it to keep track of the plants, animals, and rock formations you spot.

Here's how to keep a notebook like a real scientist, using the scientific method:

1. WHEN DID YOU START THE EXPERIMENT?
Write the date at the top of the page.

2. WHAT DO YOU WANT TO SEE OR LEARN?
Pose a question. For example, "What will happen when I mix baking soda and vinegar together in a bottle?"

3. WHAT DO YOU THINK WILL HAPPEN?
Build a hypothesis. A hypothesis is defined as a tentative explanation for an observation, phenomenon, or scientific problem that can be tested by further investigation. In other words, it's a guess about what might happen based on what you already know.

4. WHAT HAPPENED WHEN YOU DID YOUR EXPERIMENT TO TEST YOUR HYPOTHESIS?
Record your results by measuring, writing, drawing, or photographing the results. Tape photos into your notebook.

5. DID EVERYTHING GO THE WAY YOU THOUGHT IT WOULD?
Look at the information you've collected (your data) and draw a conclusion. Were the results in line with what you thought would happen? Did they support your hypothesis?

After you've done the initial experiment, think of other ways you could address the question, try some of the enrichment activities, or invent a new experiment, based on what you just did. How can what you learned be applied to the world around you? Write down your thoughts in your notebook, in case you want to come back to them some day.

CARBONATED
CHEMICAL REACTIONS

THERE ARE MANY SIMPLE CHEMICAL REACTIONS YOU CAN DO WITH INGREDIENTS YOU HAVE IN THE KITCHEN. IN FACT, EVERY TIME YOU MAKE COOKIES OR PANCAKES, YOU CREATE A CHEMICAL REACTION TO MAKE THEM RISE.

What's a chemical reaction? It's simpler than you might think.

Everything in our world is made of tiny pieces called atoms. Atoms are often connected to other atoms to form groups of linked atoms called molecules. A water molecule, for example, has two hydrogen atoms and one oxygen atom, bonded together.

A chemical reaction occurs when you mix two different kinds of molecules together to make one or more new kinds of molecules. In other words, it's just mixing two things together to make something new. You can often tell chemical reactions are happening when you see bubbles, feel a temperature difference, notice an odor, or watch a color change.

This unit contains fun chemical reactions that let you mix things together to make carbon dioxide gas.

COLOR-CHANGING MAGIC POTION

MATERIALS

→ Head of red cabbage

→ Knife

→ Pot

→ Blender (optional, see note)

→ Water

→ Heatproof spoon

→ Clear glasses, jars, or small bowls

→ Colander

→ White paper towels

→ 1 heaping teaspoon (5 g) baking soda

→ 3 tablespoons (45 ml) white vinegar

SAFETY TIPS & HINTS

An adult should boil the cabbage and strain the hot liquid.

This experiment may overflow, so have the paper towels ready.

MAKE RED CABBAGE JUICE CHANGE COLOR AND FOAM OVER IN THIS BRILLIANT, BUBBLY EXPERIMENT.

Fig. 5: The bubbles contain carbon dioxide gas.

PROTOCOL

STEP 1: Chop a head of red cabbage into small pieces and place it in a pot with enough water to cover it completely.

STEP 2: Boil the cabbage uncovered for about 15 minutes, stirring occasionally.

STEP 3: Remove from the heat, let the juice cool, and strain the purple juice into a jar or bowl. Pour about ¼ cup (60 ml) of the cabbage juice, or "magic potion," into each of two clear glasses, jars, or bowls and set them on a white paper towel.

STEP 4: Add the baking soda to one glass of cabbage juice and stir. Observe the color change. (Fig. 1)

. 1: Add the baking soda to one ss of cabbage juice.

Fig. 2: Add the vinegar to the other glass of cabbage juice.

Fig. 3: Pour the pink cabbage juice into the blue cabbage juice.

Fig. 4: Watch the chemical reaction.

TEP 5: To the second glass, add the vinegar and see what olor it turns. (Fig. 2)

TEP 6: Pour the glass of cabbage juice containing vinegar ink) into the glass of cabbage juice containing the baking oda (blue/green). (Fig. 3)

Note: To avoid needing to use the stove, chop half of a head of red cabbage and blend it in a blender with about 3 cups (710 ml) of water. Strain the liquid through a colander and then through a coffee filter in a plastic bag with one corner cut off. Blended cabbage juice makes longer-lasting bubbles and turns a slightly brighter shade of blue.

THE SCIENCE BEHIND THE FUN:

Pigments are molecules that give things color. The pigments in red cabbage juice change shape and absorb light differently depending on whether they're exposed to an acid or base. This makes them change color, so we call them acid-base indicators.

Vinegar is an acid and turns the potion pink. Baking soda is a base, which turns the pigment in cabbage juice blue or green.

When you mix the juice containing vinegar and the juice with baking soda together, a chemical reaction occurs. One product of the reaction is carbon dioxide gas, which makes your solution foam.

CREATIVE ENRICHMENT

Try adding some other liquids to your magic potion. Can you tell whether they're acids or bases?

PAPER BAG VOLCANO

MATERIALS

→ Paper lunch sack or small paper bag

→ Scissors (optional)

→ Tape

→ Empty plastic water or soda bottle

→ White vinegar

→ Food coloring

→ ¼ cup (55 g) baking soda (plus more for step 9)

SAFETY TIPS & HINTS

Vinegar can sting your eyes.

Don't worry about making your volcano perfect. It will get soaked!

MAKE A KITCHEN-TABLE KRAKATOA.

PROTOCOL

STEP 1: Invert the brown paper bag and cut or tear a small triangle off one corner to form a hole. This will be the mouth of your volcano.

STEP 2: Tear, cut, fold, crumple, and tape the bag to form a cone shape that will sit over the bottle, with the mouth of the bottle sticking through the cut corner of the bag, but don't tape the bag to the bottle. Decorate your volcano.

STEP 3: Remove the bottle from the bag and fill it halfway full of vinegar. (Fig. 1)

STEP 4: Add several drops of food coloring to your "lava." (Fig. 2)

STEP 5: Place the bag back over the bottle to hide the lava container.

Fig. 1: Add vinegar to the bottle.

STEP 6: Tape a piece of paper together to form a cone with a hole on one end that will fit inside the mouth of your volcano. You'll use this as a funnel to add the baking soda.

STEP 7: Place the volcano in a tray or container to contain the overflow.

Fig. 2: Use food coloring to tint your lava.

STEP 8: Start the eruption by quickly pouring ¼ cup (55 g) of baking soda through the cone into the volcano. Remove the cone immediately. (Fig. 3, 4)

STEP 9: When your volcano stops erupting, try adding more baking soda to see what happens.

Fig. 3: Pour the baking soda into your volcano.

Fig. 4: Stand back!

THE SCIENCE
BEHIND THE FUN:

The volcano you constructed erupts when the baking soda combines with the vinegar to produce bubbles of carbon dioxide gas, which is one of the gases spewed by real volcanoes.

Real volcanoes erupt with much greater force. When Krakatoa erupted in 1883, the explosion and resulting tsunamis killed around forty thousand people, forever changed the geography of the East Indies, spewed tons of sulfur dioxide and ash into the atmosphere, and resulted in some of the most spectacular sunsets in recorded history.

CREATIVE
ENRICHMENT

How much baking soda do you have to add to one cup (235 ml) of vinegar until it stops foaming?

LAB 03

FIZZY BALLOONS

MATERIALS

→ Medium-sized balloon

→ An empty 16 oz soda or water bottle

→ ⅓ cup (80 ml) vinegar

→ 3 teaspoons (14 g) baking soda

→ Spoon

WATCH A BUBBLY CHEMICAL REACTION INFLATE A BALLOON WITH INVISIBLE CARBON DIOXIDE GAS.

PROTOCOL

STEP 1: Pour ⅓ cup (80 ml) vinegar into the soda bottle.

STEP 2: Hold the mouth of the balloon open and use a spoon to pour 3 teaspoon (14 g) or so of baking soda into the balloon. This takes two people, one to hold the balloon open and one to add the soda. (Fig. 1)

SAFETY
TIPS & HINTS

It's a good idea to wear safety goggles or sunglasses to protect your eyes, since vinegar is a mild acid and can sting if the balloon accidentally shoots off the bottle.

STEP 3: Shake the soda down into the "bulb" or the main part of the balloon. Carefully stretch the mouth of the balloon completely over the mouth of the bottle, keeping the main part of the balloon off to one side, so the baking soda isn't dumped into the bottle until you're ready. (Fig. 2)

STEP 4: Holding the mouth of the balloon on the bottle, shake the soda into the bottle, all at once. (Fig. 3)

Fig. 1: Add baking soda to the balloon with a helper.

Fig. 2: Put the mouth of the balloon over the bottle's mouth, but keep the baking soda off to one side.

Fig. 3: Shake the baking soda into the bottle quickly, all at once.

THE SCIENCE
BEHIND THE FUN:

The scientific name for baking soda is *sodium bicarbonate*. Kitchen vinegar is diluted *acetic acid*. When mixed together, these two chemicals react to form some new chemicals, including carbon dioxide gas, which inflates the balloon. We know a reaction is happening because we can see bubbles forming, the bottle feels cold, and the balloon inflates with the invisible gas.

CREATIVE
ENRICHMENT

What happens if you use another method to generate carbon dioxide gas? Many living organisms, including humans, produce carbon dioxide gas when they break down nutrients. Could you do a similar experiment using baker's yeast, sugar, and water to inflate the balloon? Do you think it would take longer?

For tips on growing yeast, see Lab 15, "Yeast Garden."

FRANKENWORMS

MATERIALS

→ Gummy worms candy

→ Scissors or kitchen shears

→ 3 tablespoons (42 g) baking soda

→ 1 cup (235 ml) warm water

→ Spoon

→ Jar or clear drinking glass

→ White vinegar

→ Fork

BRING GUMMY WORMS TO "LIFE" WITH A SIMPLE CHEMICAL REACTION.

Fig. 5: Watch them wriggle and float.

SAFETY
TIPS & HINTS

To avoid cuts and frustration, help young kids cut the gummy worms into long strips.

PROTOCOL

STEP 1: Using scissors or kitchen shears, make super-skinny gummy worms by cutting them into long strips. Cut each worm lengthwise at least four times. The skinnier you make your worms, the better they'll work. (Fig. 1, 2)

STEP 2: Mix the baking soda with the warm water. Stir well. Drop your skinny gummy worms into the baking soda solution. Let them soak for 15 to 20 minutes. (Fig. 3)

STEP 3: While your worms are soaking, fill a clear glass or jar with vinegar.

STEP 4: When the 20 minutes are up, fish the gummy worms out of the baking soda solution with a fork and drop them into the glass of vinegar to bring them to "life." (Fig. 4, 5)

Fig. 1: Cut the gummy worms into very thin strips.

Fig. 2: The thinner they are, the better they'll work.

Fig. 3: Soak your gummy worms in the baking soda solution.

Fig. 4: Drop the baking soda–soaked worms into the vinegar.

THE SCIENCE
BEHIND THE FUN:

The gummy worms float and move as the vinegar (acetic acid) in the cup reacts with the baking soda (sodium bicarbonate) you've soaked them in to form carbon dioxide gas bubbles. The gas bubbles are less dense than the vinegar and will float to the surface, pulling the worms with them. This makes the gummy worms wriggle until the chemical reaction stops.

CREATIVE
ENRICHMENT

Why don't full-size gummy worms work well for this experiment? What else could you bring to "life" with this chemical reaction?

SODA GEYSER

MATERIALS

→ 1 (2 L) bottle Diet Coke

→ Sheet of paper

→ Roll of Mentos mints

CREATE A FOUNTAIN OF FOAM WITH SODA AND MINTS.

SAFETY
TIPS & HINTS

Wear glasses or safety goggles and stand back after adding the mints or you might get soaked. Do this experiment outdoors.

PROTOCOL

STEP 1: Remove the lid from the Diet Coke and set the bottle on a flat surface.

STEP 2: Roll the paper into a tube so it will just fit into the mouth of the bottle. The tube must be big enough to hold the mints. (Fig. 1)

STEP 3: Put your finger over the hole in the bottom of the tube and fill it with the mints. (Fig. 2)

STEP 4: Quickly empty the mints, all at once, from the paper tube into the bottle and stand back! (Fig. 3, 4, 5)

Fig. 1: Make a paper tube for the mints.

Fig. 2: Fill the tube with mints.

Fig. 3: Empty the mints from the tube into the bottle.

Fig. 4: The mints will react with the Diet Coke to make carbon dioxide gas.

Fig. 5: Stand back!

THE SCIENCE
BEHIND THE FUN:

Scientists think the sweetener and other chemicals in the Diet Coke react with chemicals in the Mentos mints. Carbon dioxide bubbles from the reaction form very quickly on all the tiny holes on the rough, pitted surface of the candy. This causes an enormous release of carbon dioxide bubbles that builds pressure in the bottle and sends a jet of soda and bubbles shooting into the air.

CREATIVE
ENRICHMENT

How well does this experiment work with different sodas or mints? Will it work with fruit Mentos?

CRYSTAL GARDENS

WE LIVE IN A WORLD OF INSTANT GRATIFICATION. GROWING CRYSTALS TEACHES KIDS THAT YOU CAN'T RUSH NATURE. ALTHOUGH CRYSTALS CAN TAKE WEEKS TO GROW, SUCH PROJECTS AS MAKING ROCK CANDY CAN HAVE A GREAT PAYOFF AT THE END.

Crystals are geometric grids of atoms. Imagine a three-dimensional chain-link fence and you'll get the picture. From the salt crystals on your table to the silicon crystals that make up semiconductors, LED displays, and solar cells, we depend on these ordered networks of molecules to enhance our lives.

In this unit, you'll use supersaturated solutions to grow two types of crystals: alum and sugar. All of the ingredients can be picked up at your local grocery store, if you don't already have them on hand.

ALUM CRYSTALS

MATERIALS

→ ¾ cup (160 g) alum (potassium aluminum sulfate [see note]), plus more for sprinkling, from the spice section of the grocery store.

→ 3 whole raw eggs

→ Serrated knife

→ Small paintbrush or cotton swab

→ Glue

→ 2 cups (475 ml) water

→ Small pot, to boil the water

→ Food coloring (optional)

CREATE SPARKLING GEODES BY USING ALUM POWDER AND EGGSHELLS.

Fig. 5: Remove you *eggshell from the* *alum solution and c*

SAFETY
TIPS & HINTS

An adult should cut the eggshells in half and boil the crystals

Always wash your hands after handling raw eggs.

PROTOCOL

STEP 1: Using a serrated knife, cut the eggs in half lengthwise and rinse them out. Let the eggshells dry.

STEP 2. Apply a thin layer of glue to the inside of an eggshell, using a paintbrush or cotton swab. (Fig. 1) Sprinkle alum powder on the wet glue and let your eggs dry overnight. (Fig. 2)

STEP 3: Dissolve the ¾ cup (160 g) of alum in the water by boiling the mixture in a small pot. This step requires adult supervision. Make sure all the alum dissolves (it may still look a little cloudy) and let the solution cool. This is your supersaturated alum solution.

Fig. 1: Paint the inside of an eggshell with glue.

Fig. 2: Sprinkle alum crystals on the wet glue.

Fig. 3: Add the alum to the water and boil to dissolve.

Fig. 4: Submerge the "seeded" eggshell in the cool alum solution.

STEP 4: When the solution is cool enough to be safely handled, gently immerse your eggshell in the alum solution. For color, you can add a large squirt of food coloring. (Fig. 4)

STEP 5: Let your project sit undisturbed to grow crystals.

STEP 6: After three days, gently remove your object from the alum solution and let it dry. (Fig. 5)

NOTE: Alum can be found in the spice section of a grocery store or supermarket. Usually four or five small jars will do the trick.

THE SCIENCE
BEHIND THE FUN:

Alum, also called potassium aluminum sulfate, is found in baking powder and is used in making pickles. Some crystals, such as alum, will form from supersaturated solutions.

A supersaturated solution is one that is forced to hold more atoms in water (or another solute) than it normally would. You can make these solutions at home by heating the solution and then allowing it to cool.

Crystals can form when a supersaturated solution encounters a "seed" atom or molecule, causing the other atoms to come out of the solution and attach to the seed. In this experiment, crystals grow on the seeds of alum you sprinkled into the glue.

CREATIVE
ENRICHMENT

Could you do the same experiment with salt or sugar crystals? How do you think the color gets incorporated into the crystal? Do you think the food coloring disrupts the shape? Will larger crystals grow if you let your object sit in the solution longer?

Try coating other objects with glue and growing crystals on them.

ROCK CANDY

MATERIALS

→ 5 cups (1 kg) white granulated sugar (plus more for step 1)

→ 2 cups (470 ml) water

→ Cake-pop sticks or wooden skewers

→ Medium-size pot, to boil the water

→ Glass containers

→ Food coloring

GROW COLORFUL, DELICIOUS SUGAR CRYSTALS ON A STICK.

SAFETY
TIPS & HINTS

This experiment requires adult supervision for boiling and handling the hot sugar syrup. Once it's cooled down, the kids can take over.

PROTOCOL

STEP 1: Dip one end of the cake-pop sticks or wooden skewers in water and then roll them in the sugar. The sugar should cover 2 to 3 inches (5 to 7.5 cm) of the sticks. Let them dry completely. These are the seeds for the sugar crystal growth. (Fig. 1)

STEP 2: Boil the 2 cups of water and the 5 cups sugar in a medium-size pot until the sugar is dissolved as much as possible. It should look like syrup. Once cool, this is your supersaturated sugar solution.

Fig. 1: Roll the ends of the sticks sugar.

Fig. 2: Add food coloring to syrup and stir.

Fig. 3: Remove the candy from the syrup.

STEP 3: Let the syrup sit until it is no longer hot, and pour into glass containers. Add food coloring and stir. (Fig. 2)

STEP 4: When the colored syrup has cooled to room temperature, set the sugary end of the sugar-seeded cake-pop sticks or skewers into the syrup and let them sit for about a week. Gently move the sticks around occasionally, so they don't stick to the crystals in the bottom of the glass. If the glass container gets too full of crystals, pour the syrup into a new container and move your stick into the clear syrup to grow more crystals.

STEP 5: When the rock candy is done, drain the excess syrup and let the sticks dry. Look at them under a magnifying glass for a close-up look. (Fig. 3)

STEP 6: Bon appétit!

THE SCIENCE
BEHIND THE FUN:

Like bricks in a wall, crystals are solids formed by a network of repeating patterns of molecules. Instead of the mortar that holds brick together, the atoms and molecules are connected by atomic bonds.

Crystals that share the same chemical composition can be big or small, but the molecules always come together to form the same shape. Table sugar, or sucrose, is made up of a molecule comprised of two sugars, glucose and fructose. Crystals formed by sucrose are hexagonal (six-sided) prisms, slanted at the ends.

The crystals that make up your rock candy grow larger when the sugar molecules in the syrup bind to the seed crystals of sugar that you rolled onto the stick.

CREATIVE
ENRICHMENT

What other surfaces could you grow sugar crystals on? How big will they get? If you leave your rock candy in sugar solution for months, will the crystals continue to grow?

UNIT
03

PHYSICS, MOTION, AND ROCKETS

MANY YEARS AGO IN ENGLAND, THERE WAS A STUDENT WHO LOVED MATH AND SCIENCE. HE STUDIED THE WORK OF GREAT THINKERS, SUCH AS COPERNICUS, GALILEO, AND KEPLER, AND OBSERVED THE WORLD AROUND HIM WITH CURIOSITY AND WONDER.

Legend has it that he saw an apple fall from a tree and came up with the idea of gravity, which gave him a new way to think about the motion of planets. This scholar, whose name was Sir Isaac Newton, published a book in 1687 about motion and gravitation that changed the way people saw the world, the universe, and science in general.

In physics, the motion of an object is defined as a change in location or position with respect to time. A change in motion is the result of some force applied to that object. In this unit, you'll play with motion, force, and energy to see how they affect everyday objects.

TABLECLOTH TRICK

MATERIALS

→ Table

→ Sturdy, heavy bowl or drinking glass that isn't too tall or tippy

→ Seamless tablecloth, easel paper, or old bedsheet with the seams cut off

→ Water

This is a fun experiment to do outside, since it can take a little practice. Having grass or a soft blanket under the table helps prevent dishes from breaking.

AMAZE YOUR FRIENDS AND FAMILY WITH THIS FEAT OF PHYSICS.

Fig. 3: Ta da

PROTOCOL

STEP 1: Put the tablecloth on the table so it covers about 2 feet (61 cm) of the flat surface.

STEP 2: Fill the bowl or glass halfway full with water and place it on the tablecloth near the edge of the table.

STEP 3: Grasping the tablecloth with two hands, pull it straight down, along the edge of the table, very fast. This is important. If you pull it out, toward you, or pull it too slowly, it won't work. If you do it correctly, the water will slosh a little, but the bowl or glass will remain on the table, full of water. (Fig. 1, 2, 3)

g. 1: Pull the tablecloth upward to prepare.

Fig. 2: Pull straight down, very fast.

THE SCIENCE BEHIND THE FUN:

The law of inertia says that objects don't want to change the speed at which they're moving (or not moving, in the case of our water glass). The heavier something is, the more inertia it has.

In this experiment, the heavy glass of water is standing still and doesn't want to move. Since the tablecloth is moving under the glass very quickly, the heavy glass slips on it, but doesn't move very far. Even the friction between the glass and the tablecloth isn't a strong enough force to make it move. It might seem like magic, but it's physics.

What happens if you do this with a heavy plate and silverware? What material works best for the tablecloth? What doesn't work?

EGG-THROWING EXPERIMENT

MATERIALS

→ An old sheet

→ Clothespins, twisty-ties, or string

→ Raw eggs

→ Tree, clothesline, or 2 people to hold the sheet

→ 2 chairs

NEXT TO THE KITCHEN TABLE, THE BACKYARD IS OUR FAVORITE SCIENCE LABORATORY. LEARN ABOUT MOTION AND FORCE BY THROWING EGGS.

SAFETY TIPS & HINTS

Always wash your hands after handling raw eggs. They can have unhealthy bacteria called *Salmonella* living in them and on them.

PROTOCOL

STEP 1: Hang the sheet from a tree by attaching it to branches using clothespins, twisty-ties, or string. If you don't have a tree, hang the sheet from something else, or have two assistants hold it up.

STEP 2: Have two people hold the bottom of the sheet up to form a J shape, or tie it to two chairs. (Fig. 1)

STEP 3: Throw a raw egg at the sheet as hard as you can. It won't break because the sheet slows the movement of the egg as it comes to a stop. (Fig. 2)

Fig. 1: (above) Have two people hold the bottom of the sheet up to form a J shape.

Fig. 2: (left) Throw the eggs at the middle of the sheet as hard as you can.

Fig. 3: The eggs will not break.

CREATIVE ENRICHMENT

What happens if you change the speed of the egg quickly, with lots of force? Tape newspaper to the side of your garage or to a table turned on its side. Throw an egg at the hard surface. Don't forget to clean up! A garden hose should do the trick.

THE SCIENCE BEHIND THE FUN:

An object in motion wants to remain in motion. To stop an egg that's moving through the air, you have to apply force to the egg. In this experiment, the force is applied by a hanging sheet.

The law of motion says that the faster you change the speed of an object, the greater the force applied to the object will be. When you change the speed of the egg slowly, like the sheet does, it lessens the force applied to the egg and the egg remains intact.

This is why they put airbags in cars. If a car is moving and hits something, causing it to stop very quickly, the airbag acts like the sheet, slowing the person in the car down SLOWLY and greatly reducing the amount of force with which they hit the dashboard.

EASY STRAW ROCKETS

MATERIALS

→ Printer paper

→ Ruler

→ Scissors

→ Pencil

→ Plastic drinking straw

→ Tape

SAFETY
TIPS & HINTS

Young kids may need help taping their rockets.

DESIGN THE ULTIMATE BREATH-PROPELLED PROJECTILE.

Fig. 3: Use your breath to propel your rocket into the air.

PROTOCOL

STEP 1: For the body of your rocket, cut a strip of paper 2 inches (5 cm) wide and 8 ½ inches (21.5 cm) long.

STEP 2: Wrap the rectangle of paper around a pencil the long way and tape it well, so it holds its shape. (Fig. 1)

STEP 3: Remove your rocket from the pencil, fold one end over, and tape it down. This will be the nose of your rocket.

Fig. 1: Roll and tape paper around a pencil.

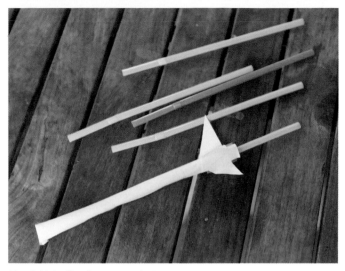

Fig. 2: Make fins for your rocket.

STEP 4: Cut triangles from paper to make fins and tape them on the bottom of your rocket, opposite the nose. Fins work best taped on at right angles, or near right angles. (Fig. 2)

STEP 5: Decorate your rocket with markers.

STEP 6: Put your rocket over the end of a straw and use the force of your breath to launch it. (Fig. 3)

THE SCIENCE
BEHIND THE FUN:

Paper rockets demonstrate how real rockets fly through the atmosphere.

Drag is the force of air getting in the way of your rocket. Weight also drags your rocket down as gravity pulls on it. The lighter you make your rocket (less paper, less tape), and the less drag it has, the farther it will go!

Fins stabilize a rocket's flight. The size and design of the fins affect how well it can be controlled.

CREATIVE
ENRICHMENT

Record your flight lengths. How far does your rocket fly? Try making longer and shorter rockets to see how flight length is affected. What happens if you change the shape or number of fins? How does the angle of your launch affect the flight trajectory?

SKY-HIGH BOTTLE ROCKETS

MATERIALS

→ Cardboard box, such as a shoebox

→ Scissors

→ 1 or 2 liter-size plastic bottles from a carbonated beverage

→ Cork that will fit in the mouth of the plastic bottle

→ Serrated knife

→ Water

→ Needle for inflating balls

→ Bike or ball pump

SAFETY
TIPS & HINTS

These rockets fly far and fast, so shoot them off in an open area with adult supervision.

When you put your rocket on the launch pad, make sure the cork end of the bottle is pointed down and the bottom of the bottle points up. Wear eye protection and make sure that everyone is standing well behind the rocket before you pump air into the bottles.

HAVE A BLAST LEARNING PHYSIC AS YOU LAUNCH BOTTLE ROCKETS, USING WATER AND A BIKE PUMP.

Fig. 5: As air pressure pushes the cork and water out of the bottle, the rocket takes off in the opposite direction.

PROTOCOL

STEP 1: Make a launch pad by cutting the cardboard box so that it will hold the bottle upside down, at about a 45-degree angle. The inflating end of the bike pump must have access to the mouth of the bottle.

STEP 2: Find a cork that will fit your plastic bottle. Have an adult carefully cut the cork in half with a serrated knife. Push the inflation needle through one half of the cork until it pokes out of the opposite side. Use the hole from the corkscrew as a guide, to make it easier. (Fig. 1)

STEP 3: Fill the plastic bottle about two-thirds of the way full of water, attach the needle to the bike pump, and insert the cork in the bottle. (Fig. 2)

Fig. 1: Push an inflation needle through half a cork.

Fig. 2: Fill the bottle two-thirds of the way with water.

Fig. 3: Set the bottle in the launch pad with the bottom of the bottle pointing up and away from you.

STEP 4: Set the bottle, cork side down, in the cardboard box so that the bottom of the bottle is pointing up, but away from you. (Fig. 3)

STEP 5: Stand behind the launch pad, put your safety goggles on, and prepare for blastoff. (Fig. 4)

STEP 6: Start pumping air into the bottle. The air pressure will build in the bubble at the top of the rocket. When the pressure gets high enough, it will force the cork and water out of the bottom of the bottle with lots of force. As the water shoots down, the rocket will shoot up! (Fig. 5, 6)

Fig. 4: Start pumping air into the bottle.

Fig. 6: Blast off!

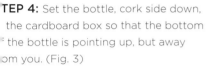 # THE SCIENCE
BEHIND THE FUN:

Although these rockets lack fins, a payload, and a nose cone, they're very similar to real rockets. Whereas NASA's rockets use rocket fuel as their working mass, these rockets use water. As pressurized air forces the water out of your rocket, the rocket moves in the opposite direction, just as Newton's Third Law says it will: "For every action, there is an equal and opposite reaction."

CREATIVE ENRICHMENT

What happens if you add more or less water to your rocket?

LIFE SCIENCE LABS

LIVING THINGS ARE MARVELOUS MOSAICS OF MOLECULES. RESEARCHERS WHO STUDY THE COMPLEXITIES OF LIVING SYSTEMS HOPE TO MAKE DISCOVERIES THAT WILL MAKE THE WORLD A HAPPIER, HEALTHIER PLACE FOR ALL LIVING CREATURES, INCLUDING US.

From chicken eggs to DNA, it's fun to explore the science of life at home. This unit investigates eggshells, demonstrating how the amazing architecture of life can be strong and fragile at the same time. You'll also learn how to lift fingerprints using transparent tape. While our DNA makes each of us unique at a molecular level, our fingerprints are physical manifestations of our individuality.

ALIEN MONSTER EGGS

MATERIALS

→ Jar large enough to hold your eggs

→ Whole raw eggs (in the shell)

→ Permanent markers (optional)

→ White or cider vinegar

→ Green food coloring

→ Corn syrup

Remember to always wash your hands after handling raw eggs because some carry bacteria that can make you sick!

Be careful not to get vinegar in your eyes since vinegar is a mild acid and stings!

DISSOLVE EGGSHELLS WITH VINEGAR AND USE CORN SYRUP TO SHRIVEL YOUR MONSTROUS CREATIONS.

PROTOCOL

STEP 1: Put some whole raw eggs into a jar and cover them with vinegar. It's fun to use permanent markers to make the eggs look like eyeballs before you put them in the vinegar. (Fig. 1)

STEP 2: Let the eggs sit overnight in the refrigerator. Gently rinse them with water. Only the membrane of the egg will remain, which is like a rubbery balloon. How does it feel? (Fig. 2)

STEP 3: To make alien monster eggs, dump out the vinegar, rinse the eggs, and return them to the jar. Cover them with corn syrup and add some green food coloring. Gently invert the jar to mix. Leave them for 24 hours in the refrigerator. How do they look? (Fig. 3, 4)

Fig. 1: Put whole raw eggs into a jar and cover with vinegar.

Fig. 2: Remove the eggs from the vinegar the next day and observe them.

Fig. 3: Rinse the eggs and add corn syrup.

Fig. 4: Corn syrup will shrivel the eggs.

THE SCIENCE
BEHIND THE FUN:

Eggshells are made up of two chemical elements called calcium and carbon, which are bound together in calcium carbonate crystals. Vinegar is an acid that breaks the crystals apart in a chemical reaction. The calcium carbonate and vinegar react to form carbon dioxide bubbles, which you see when you add vinegar to the eggs.

The balloonlike membrane of eggs allows water molecules to pass through. Corn syrup is mostly sugar and doesn't have much water in it, so water molecules move out of the egg into the corn syrup, causing the egg to shrivel.

CREATIVE
ENRICHMENT

Rinse the eggs and submerge them in water again overnight (in the fridge). What happens?

FINGERPRINTING LAB

MATERIALS

→ 2 sheets of white paper

→ Transparent tape, such as Scotch Tape

→ Pencil

→ Magnifying glass

→ Clear glass or jar

→ Unsweetened cocoa powder

→ A paintbrush or makeup brush

SAFETY TIPS & HINTS

Be very gentle when dusting prints so you don't smear the image.

DUST FOR FINGERPRINTS AND TRY YOUR HAND AT DERMATOGLYPHICS.

PROTOCOL

STEP 1: On one sheet of paper, trace your left hand with a pencil. If you're left-handed, trace your right hand. (Fig. 1)

STEP 2: On the other piece of paper, scribble hard with the pencil until a small area is covered with the graphite from the pencil lead. Rub your pinkie around in the graphite until it is covered with gray. Carefully place your graphite-covered pinkie finger on the sticky side of a piece of transparent tape and gently lift your finger off the tape. A clear fingerprint should be visible. (Fig. 2)

STEP 3: Place the tape facedown on the pinkie finger of the hand you traced.

g. 1: Trace your hand with a
encil.

Fig. 2: Transfer your graphite
fingerprint to clear tape.

Fig. 3: Tape your fingerprints to
the matching fingers on your
traced hand.

Fig. 4: Inspect your fingerprints.

STEP 4: Repeat with each finger of your left hand until you
ave fingerprints on each of the five fingers you traced. (Fig. 3)

STEP 5: Inspect the fingerprints under a magnifying glass, or
ith your naked eye. (Fig. 4)

STEP 6:. Rub your hands together to spread the oil on your
kin around, then make several fingerprints on a clear glass.

STEP 7: Using a brush, gently dust some cocoa powder onto
ne of the fingerprints on the glass.

STEP 8: Blow the excess cocoa powder away and lift the
fingerprint with a piece of tape.

STEP 9: Tape the fingerprint onto a piece of white paper
and try to match it to one from your hand. Can you figure out
which finger it came from?

THE SCIENCE
BEHIND THE FUN:

Skin's outer layer is called the epidermis, and a
fingerprint is the impression left by epidermal ridges on
human fingers. These ridges help us feel things and grip
things better. No two people have identical fingerprints,
although fingerprint patterns tend to run in families.
These patterns tend to look like whorls, loops, or arches,
and fingers often leave imprints of sweat, oil, ink, or
other substances behind. Fingerprints are often essential
tools in crime scene investigations and the scientific
study of fingerprints is called dermatoglyphics.

CREATIVE
ENRICHMENT

Make a fingerprint profile for your family members
and dust the water glasses from your table after dinner.
Can you identify who used each glass?

Try dusting your fingertips with cornstarch, lifting the
prints with tape and taping them onto black paper. How
do they compare to the ones you lifted using graphite?

MICROBE ZOO

MATERIALS

→ Clean, disposable containers, such as individual foil muffin tins or clear plastic cups covered with resealable plastic bags, clear plastic ware with lids, or petri dishes

→ Small pot or microwavable bowl

→ Beef bouillon cubes or 1 teaspoon (about 2 g) granules

→ 1 cup (235 ml) water

→ 1 tablespoon (14 g) powdered agar-agar or 1 ½ envelopes (0.5-ounce [12 g]) unflavored gelatin (see note)

→ 2 teaspoons (9 g) sugar

→ Plate or plastic wrap

→ Cotton swabs

→ Pen and labels

WHAT'S ON YOUR KITCHEN COUNTER? GROW COLONIES FROM SOME OF THE MICROBES LIVING AROUND YOUR HOME.

Fig. 4: See what grows!

SAFETY TIPS & HINTS

Making the plates requires handling very hot liquids, so adult assistance is required.

If you use foil muffin cups as your petri dishes, simply place them in a muffin pan, fill them with agar-agar, and when they're cool, put them in individual resealable plastic bags.

Plates should be used in two to three days. When you're working with them, try to keep the lids on loosely whenever possible, so that they're not contaminated by microorganisms floating around in the air.

Wash your hands after handling the plates, and throw them away when you're finished observing them.

PROTOCOL

STEP 1: To make the microbe food, or microbial growth medium, mix the beef bouillon, water, agar-agar or gelatin, and sugar together in a small pot or microwavable bowl. (Fig. 1)

STEP 2: Bring the mixture to a boil on the stove, stirring at 1-minute intervals and watching carefully until the agar-agar or gelatin is dissolved. Remove boiling liquid from the heat and cover with a plate or plastic wrap. Let cool for about 15 minutes.

STEP 3: Pour the medium carefully into the clean containers, about one-third full. Loosely place lids, or plastic bags over the containers and allow them to cool completely. When the portions of the mixture are solid, they're ready to use or store (sealed) in a refrigerator. (Fig. 2)

. 1: Mix together ingredients.

Fig. 2: Pour plates.

Fig. 3: Take samples by swabbing surfaces.

EP 4: Shake the condensation (water droplets) off the lids of the containers d replace the lids. Label the bottom of each container with the date and name the surface you want to test. Use a separate container for each surface or divide ch plate into four sections and label each section.

EP 5: Test surfaces by rubbing a clean cotton swab around on the surface you nt to test. Remove the lid from the container labeled with the name of that face and gently rub the swab across the section of the plate labeled for that face. Phones, remote controls, kitchen sinks, computer keyboards, doorknobs, d piano keys are great surfaces to check. You can even touch your finger to the ate, cough on a plate, or leave one open to the air for half an hour to see what's ating around. (Fig. 3)

EP 7: When you're done swabbing, set the plates on a flat surface with their s loosened and taped on.

STEP 8: Observe your plates to see what grows. You'll mostly see fungi (molds), but you may also see some tiny clear or white spots that are colonies formed by millions of bacteria. (Fig. 4) Note the shapes, sizes, and colors of the microbial colonies that grow on your plates.

Note: Gelatin will melt if it gets too warm, and some strains of bacteria can liquefy it, which is why scientists in labs use agar-agar to make their plates. Agar-agar is made from algae and can be found in the Asian food section of many grocery stores.

THE SCIENCE
BEHIND THE FUN:

Although you can't see them without a microscope, microbes, such as fungi and bacteria, live on your body and every surface you see around you. Some of them can be grown on the microbial growth media in this experiment. Like animals in a zoo, each microbe has its own particular requirements for food, moisture, temperature, and even how much air it gets. The colonies you grow must use the food and temperature you provide for them.

Colony size, color, and other characteristics can help identify what's growing on your plates. Microbiologists use microscopy, staining, chemical tests, and even nucleic acid analysis to identify unknown organisms.

YEAST GARDEN

MATERIALS

→ Small resealable plastic bags

→ Pen

→ 4 (2 ¼-teaspoon [9 g]) packages active dry yeast

→ 1 teaspoon (6 g) salt

→ 6 teaspoons (27 g) sugar

→ 2 cups (475 ml) water

Fig. 3: Add sugar to the bags you've labeled "Sugar."

MAKE YEAST BALLOONS TO DISCOVER WHAT MAKES YEAST GROW.

PROTOCOL

STEP 1: Label four resealable plastic ba_ as follows:

"Sugar + warm water"

"Sugar + cold water"

"Sugar + salt + warm water"

"No sugar + warm water" (Fig. 1)

STEP 2: Add 4 (2 ¼-teaspoon (9 g)) packages of yeast to each plastic bag. Add 2 teaspoons (9 g) of sugar to each of the three bags labeled "Sugar," and the salt to th_ bag labeled "Salt." (Fig. 2, 3)

STEP 3: Carefully, add ½ cup (120 ml) of water to each bag, according to how each b_ is labeled. The warm water should be warm, but not too hot, or it will kill the yeast. Th_ cold water can be room temperature, or you can chill it with ice. (Fig. 4)

Fig. 1: Label your plastic bags.

Fig. 2: Add yeast to each bag.

Fig. 4: Add water to each bag.

STEP 4: Seal the bags, squeezing out as much of the extra air as possible and let them sit. Yeast will grow faster in a warm room than in a cold one.

STEP 5: Watch the bags to see what happens. You will know your yeast cells are growing happily in the bag containing them puffs up as carbon dioxide gas accumulates. (Fig. 5)

Sugar + salt + warm water

Sugar + warm water

No sugar + warm water

Sugar + cold water

Fig. 5: What makes the yeast grow best?

Which ingredients help yeast grow best? Did you find an ingredient that kept them from growing well? Do yeast cells grow better in warm or cold water?

THE SCIENCE BEHIND THE FUN:

Humans have been making bread for over four thousand years. How bread rose was a mystery though, until a famous scientist named Louis Pasteur proved that tiny living organisms called yeast were responsible for making bread dough puff up.

Bread yeast is a type of fungus related to mushrooms. If you look at yeast cells under a microscope, you'll see that they're shaped like balloons and footballs. The yeast used to make bread is called *Saccharomyces cerevisiae* (sack-a-roe-MY-seas sair-a-VIS-e-ey). *Saccharomyces* means "sugar fungus."

Growing yeast cells use sugar and starches, such as the ones in bread flour, for energy. Sugar and starch-eating yeast cells produce carbon dioxide gas, which is what makes your plastic bag puff up.

In bread dough, carbon dioxide gas from yeast makes tiny bubbles that make the bread rise. They pop during baking, but leave the small holes you see in bread. The yeast you buy at the store is alive, but it is dried and can't grow until you add water to it.

CREATIVE ENRICHMENT

Try coating the yeast with oil before adding the sugar and water. What happens if you add fruit juice to the bags? What if you put the bags in the refrigerator just after adding the yeast?

VEGETABLE VAMPIRES

MATERIALS

→ 2 large cups, plastic containers, or jars, large enough to hold the base of half of your cabbage

→ Warm water

→ Food coloring

→ Head of fresh napa cabbage

→ Sharp knife

→ Fruits and veggies, such as olives and pepper, for decoration

→ Rubber bands or string

→ Toothpicks

SAFETY
TIPS & HINTS

Plan ahead. For the best result, your "vampires" will have to drink for 24 to 48 hours.

An adult should help young children cut the cabbage.

Fig. 5: Watch your cabbage vampires change color as they "drink" from the containers.

MAKE CREEPY CABBAGES DRINK FAKE BLOOD TO SEE CAPILLARY ACTION AT WOR

PROTOCOL

STEP 1: Fill your containers or jar two-thirds of the way to the top with warm (not hot) water. Add two or more drops of blue food coloring to one container and ten or more drops of red food colorin to the other one. (Fig. 1)

STEP 2: With a sharp knife, cut the cabbage in half vertically, from the bottom up, leaving the top 4 inches (10 cm) or so intact, so the two sections are still attached at the crown. If possible, try to cut down the middle of one of the big leaves, so it will turn two different colors when you do the experiment.

STEP 3: Using rubber bands or string, secure the bottom of each side of the cabbage and make a fresh cut at the bottom, about an inch (a few cm) up from the old cut. (Fig. 2)

STEP 4: Put your two cups side by side and submerge half of the base of your cabbage in the red water, and the other half in the blue water. (Fig. 3)

Fig. 1: Add a different color to each containe of water.

Fig. 2: Secure the bottom of the cut cabbage with rubber bands.

Fig. 3: Split the bottom of the cabbage into the two containers, with each half submerged in a different color water.

Fig. 4: Put eyes on your vegetable vampires.

STEP 5: Decorate your "vampires" with eyes and spooky eyebrows made from olives and peppers (or whatever you have in the refrigerator). Secure the decorations with toothpicks. (Fig. 4)

STEP 6: Check the cabbages every hour or so to see how much colored water they're drinking. (Fig. 5)

THE SCIENCE
BEHIND THE FUN:

Like vampires, plants prefer a liquid diet. They survive by drawing nutrients dissolved in water up into their stems, stalks, trunks, branches, and leaves.

Capillary action is the main force that allows the movement of water up into plants. In a narrow tube, on a surface that attracts water, the attraction between the surface and water, coupled with the attraction of the water molecules to each other, pulls water up. Plants are composed of huge numbers of tube-shaped cells that take advantage of these physical forces.

In this experiment, you can observe colored water being taken up, via capillary action, into your cabbage.

Imagine how high the water in giant redwoods must travel to reach the leaves at the top. In very tall trees, a process called transpiration helps the water overcome the forces of gravity.

CREATIVE ENRICHMENT

What happens if you use ice water for this experiment? Does adding sugar or salt affect your results? If you mix several colors together, are they all taken up at the same rate by the cabbage?

ASTONISHING MATERIALS

WHEN YOU THINK ABOUT EARTH'S IMMENSE OCEANS AND PLENTIFUL LAKES AND RIVERS, IT MIGHT SEEM AS IF THERE'S LIQUID EVERYWHERE. IF YOU'RE FORTUNATE ENOUGH TO LIVE IN A PLACE WITH GOOD SANITATION SYSTEMS, YOU CAN JUST TURN A HANDLE AND CLEAN WATER WILL POUR FROM A FAUCET.

However, because such liquids as water can only exist within a narrow range of temperatures and pressures, they're something of a rarity in the universe. In fact, most of the universe is made up of gases and plasma, with only traces of solid matter and little or no liquid.

Liquids are a type of fluid, meaning they can flow to take the shape of any container you pour them into. They exist somewhere in between solid and gaseous states and can contain multiple types of molecules. The atoms in liquids stick together due to special intermolecular glue known as cohesive forces. The interplay between forces acting on liquids are responsible for many of their interesting behaviors. In this unit, we'll play with some of the unusual properties of liquids.

TIE-DYE MILK

MATERIALS

→ Shallow dish or plate

→ Small cup or bowl

→ Milk

→ Dishwashing liquid or liquid hand soap

→ Cotton swabs

→ Liquid food coloring

SAFETY
TIPS & HINTS

Wear old clothes since food coloring stains.

YOU'LL BE AMAZED AS YOU WATCH THE FORCES OF SURFACE TENSION AT WORK IN THIS COLORFUL EXPERIMENT.

Fig. 4: Touch the milk with your swab repeatedly to make more colorful patterns.

PROTOCOL

STEP 1: Add enough milk to cover the bottom of the dish. The experiment works best with a thin layer of milk. (Fig. 1)

STEP 2: In the small cup or bowl, mix together 1 tablespoon (15 ml) of water and 1 teaspoon (5 ml) of liquid dish detergent or liquid hand soap. Some detergents may work better than others.

Fig. 1: Add milk to the dish.

Fig. 2: Add drops of food coloring to the milk.

Fig. 3: Touch the milk with your soap-soaked swab.

STEP 3: Put several drops of food coloring into the milk. Space them out in the milk so you can see what happens when you break the surface tension. (Fig. 2)

STEP 4: Dip a cotton swab into the dish soap mixture and then touch the wet swab to the milk. Don't stir! The detergent will break the surface tension of the milk and the food coloring will swirl around as if by magic. (Fig. 3)

STEP 5: You can keep re-wetting your cotton swab with soapy water and touching it to the milk. Sometimes it works to touch the swab to the bottom of the plate and hold it there for a few seconds. (Fig. 4)

THE SCIENCE
BEHIND THE FUN:

Imagine that the surface of liquids is a stretched elastic skin, like the surface of a balloon full of air. The scientific name for the way the "skin" of a liquid holds together is surface tension.

When the skin of the liquid is broken by detergent, food coloring and milk move and swirl around in interesting patterns on the milk's surface.

CREATIVE
ENRICHMENT

How does the fat content of the milk affect surface tension? Does whole milk work better than skim ?

What happens if you vary the depth of the milk in the dish?

Does the concentration of the soap matter? What happens if you put a drop of undiluted dish detergent in your milk?

RAINBOW IN A CUP

MATERIALS

→ About 2 cups (480 ml) hot tap water

→ Measuring cups and measuring spoons

→ Jars or drinking cups

→ 20 tablespoons (1 ¼ cups [260 g]) white granulated sugar

→ Food coloring

→ Tall, thin glass (such as a cordial glass) or test tube

→ Eyedropper, siphoning bulb, straw, or spoon

SAFETY TIPS & HINTS

Use caution with hot liquids.

Add the layers to the cup very slowly and carefully or they'll mix together, resulting in a muddled rainbow.

EXPLORE THE CONCEPT OF DENSITY GRADIENTS BY LAYERING A SUGAR-WATER RAINBOW.

Fig. 5: Complete your liquid rainbow.

PROTOCOL

STEP 1: Measure ½ cup (120 ml) of hot tap water into each of four jars or drinking cups. You can label your cups "2 tablespoons/red," "4 tablespoons/yellow," "6 tablespoons/green," and "8 tablespoons/blue." (Fig. 1)

STEP 2: Add 2 drops of food coloring to each jar, according to the colors they've bee labeled with. (Fig. 2)

STEP 3: To the first cup of hot water, add 2 tablespoons (26 g) of sugar.

STEP 4: To the second jar of hot water, add 4 tablespoons (52 g) of sugar.

STEP 5: To the third jar of hot water, add 6 tablespoons (78 g) of sugar. (Fig. 3)

STEP 6: To the fourth cup of hot water, add 8 tablespoons (104 g) of sugar.
By dissolving increasing amounts of sugar, you're increasing the density of the sugar-water solutions.

STEP 7: Stir each of the jars until the sugar dissolves. If the sugar won't dissolve, an adult may microwave the jar for 30 seconds and stir again. Always use caution with ho liquids. If the sugar still won't dissolve, try adding a tablespoon (15 ml) of warm water.

Fig. 1: Measure hot tap water into jars and label.

Fig. 2: Add food coloring, according to labels.

Fig. 3: Add the correct amount of sugar to each cup.

Fig. 4: Carefully add each layer, according to the directions.

STEP 8: Pour about an inch (2.5 cm) of the densest sugar solution (blue) to the bottom of your tall, thin glass or test tube.

STEP 9: Use your dropper or straw to gently drip the liquid with the next-highest density (green) on top of the blue layer. It works best to drip the sugar solution against the side of the cup just above the surface of the liquid. You can also drip it onto the back of a spoon that's set against the side of the cup.

STEP 10: Add the yellow layer in the same way. (Fig. 4)

STEP 11: Complete your rainbow with the red layer, which only contains 2 tablespoons (26 g) of sugar per ½ cup (120 ml) and is the least dense. (Fig. 5)

THE SCIENCE
BEHIND THE FUN:

Density is mass (how many atoms are in an object) divided by volume (how much space an object takes up). Sugar molecules are composed of lots of atoms stuck together. The more sugar you add to a ½ cup (120 ml) of water, the more atoms the water will contain and the denser the solution will be. Less dense liquids sit on top of denser liquids, which is why water containing only 2 tablespoons (26 g) of sugar floats on the layers that contain more sugar molecules.

Scientists sometimes use density gradients to isolate different parts of cells by breaking up the cells, putting them on top of a density gradient in a tube and spinning the tube very fast in a centrifuge. Cellular fragments of different shapes and molecular weights move through the gradient at different rates, allowing researchers to separate the cell parts they're interested in studying.

CREATIVE
ENRICHMENT

Can you make a rainbow with more layers? How long will the layers stay separated?

ICE CUBE ON A STRING

MATERIALS

→ Ice cube

→ Glass of room temperature water

→ Cotton kitchen twine or yarn

→ Scissors

→ Salt

LIFT AN ICE CUBE FROM A GLASS USING ONLY A STRING AND SOME SALT.

Fig. 1: Cut a piece of kitchen twine.

PROTOCOL

STEP 1: Cut a piece of kitchen twine about 6 inches (15 cm) long. Drop a few ice cubes into a glass of water. (Fig. 1, 2)

STEP 2: Try to pick the ice cube up by simply placing the string on top of it and pulling. Hint: Don't try too hard, because it won't work.

STEP 3: Dip the string in the water to wet it, lay it across the ice cube, and sprinkle a generous amount of salt over the string/ice cube. (Fig. 3)

STEP 4: Wait a minute or two and try again to lift the cube using only the string. This time, it should work.

ig. 2: Drop a few ice cubes into a glass of water.

Fig. 3: Sprinkle a big pinch or two of salt on the wet string sitting on an ice cube.

THE SCIENCE
BEHIND THE FUN:

Normally, ice melts and water freezes at 32°F (0°C). Adding salt, however, lowers the temperature at which ice can melt and water can freeze.

In this experiment, salt makes the ice surrounding the string begin to melt, stealing heat from the surrounding water. The cold water then refreezes around the string, which allows you to lift it from the water in the glass.

Different chemicals change the freezing point of water. Salt can thaw ice at 15°F (-9°C), but at 0°F (-18°C) it won't do anything. Other deicing chemicals they add to roads can work at much colder temperatures, down to -20°F (-29°C).

CREATIVE ENRICHMENT

Does this experiment work using sugar? What else could you try?

MAGIC BAG

MATERIALS

→ Resealable plastic bag (thick freezer bags work best)

→ Water

→ Food coloring

→ Sharp wooden or bamboo skewers

Be careful with the sharp points of the skewers. Small children should be supervised.

This is a good experiment to do outside, over a sink, or over a bowl.

DO YOU THINK A BAG OF WATER WILL LEAK IF YOU STAB IT WITH A SHARP STICK? THINK AGAIN.

Fig. 2: Push a wooden skewer in one side of the bag and out the other, through the liquid.

PROTOCOL

STEP 1: Fill the resealable plastic bag with water.

STEP 2: Add a drop or two of food coloring to the bag and seal it shut. (Fig. 1)

Fig. 1: Add food coloring to water in a resealable plastic bag and seal closed.

Fig. 3: How many skewers can you poke through your bag before it leaks?

STEP 3: Slowly poke a wooden or bamboo skewer completely through the bag, in one side, through the liquid, and out the other side. Avoid pushing it through the part of the bag containing air. (Fig. 2)

STEP 4: See how many skewers you can push through before the bag leaks. (Fig. 3)

THE SCIENCE
BEHIND THE FUN:

Plastic is a polymer, made up of long, elastic molecules that form a seal around the spot where the skewer is poking through. This polymer seal prevents the bag from leaking excessively.

CREATIVE
ENRICHMENT

Does this experiment work with other liquids? What if the water is hot, or cold? What happens if you poke one end of your stick through the portion of the bag that contains air?

MAD SCIENTIST'S SLIME

MATERIALS

→ Bowl

→ white school glue or clear glue (4–5 oz bottle)

→ Baking soda

→ Measuring cups and measuring spoons

→ Jar or bowl

→ Spoon

→ Food coloring

→ 1 cup (235 ml) warm water

→ contact lens solution containing boric acid and/or sodium borate

SAFETY
TIPS & HINTS

Slime can stick to fabric and furniture, so play with it on a table, countertop, or outside.

To do this project with several children, divide the glue solution into smaller cups and let them add a pinch of baking soda and a few squirts of contact lens solution at a time.

SYNTHESIZE A SLIMY, RUBBERY POLYMER CONCOCTION FROM GLUE, CONTACT LENS SOLUTION, AND BAKING SODA.

Fig. 3: Pull your slime out of the bowl.

PROTOCOL

STEP 1: Pour a 4–5 oz bottle of glue into a bowl.

STEP 2: Add a few drops of food coloring and stir again. This is your polymer solution. (Fig. 1)

STEP 3: Add 1 teaspoon (5 ml) of baking soda to the glue. Mix well.

STEP 4: Mix 1 tablespoon (15 ml) of contact lens solution into the glue/baking soda solution, a little bit at a time. Long strings will begin to form and stick together. Keep adding contact lens solution until the mixture doesn't feel sticky and forms a shiny rubberlike substance.

If you add too much contact lens solution, your polymer will feel wet, but you should be able to squish it around with your hands to absorb the extra solution!

STEP 5: Remove the green slime from the bowl. (Fig. 3) Roll it into long snakes or form it into bouncy balls. (Fig. 4)

Fig, 1: Mix the glue with a little food coloring. Then add baking soda and contact lens solution as directed.

Fig, 2: Add glue mixture to a bowl for everyone who wants to make slime..

Fig, 4: Roll your slime into a ball or a long snake.

THE SCIENCE
BEHIND THE FUN:

A molecule is the smallest amount of a specific chemical substance that can exist alone, such as H_2O, a single water molecule. Glue is a polymer, which is a long chain of molecules linked together like a bead necklace. In this experiment, the polymer formed by water and glue is called polyvinyl acetate.

The boric acid in contact solution combines with baking soda to make borate. Borate is called a cross-linking substance, and it makes the glue polymer chains stick to each other. As more and more chains stick together, they can't move around and the goo gets thicker and thicker. Eventually, all the chains are bound together and no more cross-linking solution can be taken up.

CREATIVE
ENRICHMENT

Play with texture! Try adding shaving cream, corn starch or lotion to the glue and baking soda solution before you add the contacts lens solution.

GELATINOUS DIFFUSION

MATERIALS

→ 4 cups (946 ml) water

→ Medium-size pot

→ 4 (1-ounce [28 g]) envelopes plain, unflavored gelatin (from the grocery store)

→ Heatproof spoon

→ Food coloring

→ Clear heatproof containers or petri dishes

→ Drinking straw

→ Toothpick

SAFETY
TIPS & HINTS

Adult supervision is required to boil water and pour the molten gelatin.

CREATE COLORFUL CIRCLES TO EXPAND YOUR UNDERSTANDING OF DIFFUSION.

Fig. 4: Measure your spots eve hour or so to see how fast the food coloring is moving throug the gelatin.

PROTOCOL

STEP 1: Boil the water in a medium-size pot. Add the gelatin to the boiling water. Stir until dissolved. Let cool slightly.

STEP 2: Pour ½ inch (1.3 cm) of liquid gelatin into the bottom of heatproof container or petri dishes, and allow it to harden. (Fig. 1)

STEP 3: Using a straw, poke several holes around ¼ inch (6 mm) deep in the gelatin. Try to avoid pushing the straw all the way through the gelatin. Remove the gelatin plugs with a toothpick. (Fig. 2)

STEP 4: Add a different-colored drop of food coloring to each hole on a plate. Do th with several plates. (Fig. 3)

STEP 5: Put one or two plates in the refrigerator and leave a few at room temperatur

STEP 6: Every so often, measure the circle of food coloring as it diffuses into the surrounding gelatin. How many centimeters per hour is it diffusing? Does the temperature make a difference? (Fig. 4, 5)

g. 1: Pour around ½ inch (1.3 cm) of liquid gelatin into veral heatproof plates.

g. 2: Use straws to make holes in the gelatin.

g. 3: Drop food coloring into each hole.

g. 5: Does the food coloring diffuse faster at room mperature, or in the refrigerator?

THE SCIENCE
BEHIND THE FUN:

Gelatin is a special substance known as a hydrocolloid, which is a suspension of tiny particles in a water-based solution. It's similar to agar-agar and is a good medium to use for diffusion experiments since it doesn't support another kind of movement in fluids, called convection.

Diffusion is the name for the way molecules move from areas of high concentration, where there are lots of other similar molecules, to areas of low concentration, where there are fewer similar molecules. When the molecules are evenly spread throughout the space, it is called equilibrium. Imagine half a box filled with yellow balls and the other half filled with blue ones. If you set the box on something that vibrates, the balls will start to move around randomly, until the blue and yellow balls are evenly mixed up.

Many things can affect how fast molecules diffuse, including temperature. When molecules are heated up, they vibrate faster and move around faster, which helps them achieve equilibrium more quickly.

Diffusion takes place in gases, liquids, and even solids, which is one way pollutants are able to move from one place to another. Bacteria take up some of the substances they need to survive using simple diffusion across their membranes. Your own body transfers oxygen, carbon dioxide, and water by processes involving diffusion as well.

CREATIVE ENRICHMENT

Do the same experiment, but make plates using 2 cups (475 ml) of red cabbage juice (see Lab 1, "Color-Changing Magic Potion"), 2 cups (475 ml) of water and 4 (1-ounce [28 g]) envelopes of gelatin. See how fast a few drops of vinegar or baking soda and water solution diffuse. A pigment in red cabbage turns pink when exposed to acid, and blue/green when exposed to a base!

CORNSTARCH GOO

MATERIALS

→ Medium-size bowl

→ Spoon (optional)

→ 1 cup + 2 tablespoons (147 g) cornstarch

→ ½ cup (120 ml) water

→ Food coloring (optional for colored goo)

SAFETY
TIPS & HINTS

Food coloring will move from the goo to hands and clothes, so beware.

For colored goo, simply add the food coloring to the water before mixing with cornstarch.

Without food coloring, this project cleans up easily with water.

MIX UP A BATCH OF NON-NEWTONIAN FUN.

Fig. 5: What happens if you stop moving it around?

PROTOCOL

STEP 1: Mix together the cornstarch, water, and food coloring in a medium-size bowl using a spoon or your fingers. The goo should be the consistency of thick syrup. (Fig. 1, 2, 3)

STEP 2: Remove some goo from the bowl and roll it into a ball. (Fig. 4)

STEP 3: Stop rolling it and let it drip between your fingers. (Fig. 5)

Fig. 1: Add the water to the cornstarch.

Fig. 2: Stir your cornstarch and water to mix.

Fig. 3: Add a little bit of food coloring to your goo.

Fig. 4: Roll the goo into a ball between your palms.

STEP 4: Put the goo on a tray or cookie sheet. What happens if you slap your hand down on it? Can you make it splash?

STEP 5: If the goo gets too dry, just add a little more water.

THE SCIENCE
BEHIND THE FUN:

Most fluids and solids behave in expected ways and hold their fluid or solid properties when you push, pull, squeeze, pour, or shake them. However, some fluids, known as non-Newtonian fluids, don't follow the rules. Cornstarch goo is one of these renegade fluids. It's called a shear-thickening non-Newtonian fluid, and when you apply stress to it, the atoms in the cornstarch rearrange to make it act more like a solid.

That's why when you let the goo sit in the palm of your hand or let it slowly slide between your fingers it looks like liquid, but if you squeeze it, stir it, or roll it around in your hands, it looks and feels more like a solid.

Someday, fluids such as these may be used to make such things as bulletproof vests that will move with the wearer but stop speeding projectiles.

CREATIVE
ENRICHMENT

What happens if you add more or less water? Does it retain the same properties? Can you think of some practical uses for non-Newtonian fluids?

SUNSHINE REQUIRED

UNTIL A FAMOUS SCIENTIST NAMED GALILEO POINTED A TELESCOPE AT THE SUN TO DISCOVER SUNSPOTS, HUMANS SAW THE SUN AS A SYMBOL OF ULTIMATE PERFECTION, A FLAWLESS GOLDEN DISK IN THE HEAVENS. GALILEO WENT ON TO RECORD HOW THE SPOTS CHANGED AND MOVED AND USED HIS DATA TO DESCRIBE THE ROTATION OF THE GIANT STAR.

Sunspots are areas of visibly reduced brightness that appear as dark spots on the sun's surface. They're caused by magnetic activity and are associated with other solar phenomena, such as flares and coronal mass ejections. You may be able to see sunspots with the solar viewer you can build by using the binoculars in Lab 48.

The sun produces an enormous amount of energy in the form of solar radiation, which warms Earth. Without the sun's energy and the greenhouse gases that blanket Earth to hold some of the energy in, there would be no life here. However, there is a delicate balance between absorbed energy and emitted energy, and since the Industrial Revolution, it's been getting more difficult for Earth to cool itself.

This unit explores the sun and the ability of solar energy to warm everything from water to marshmallows.

WINDOW SPROUTS

MATERIALS

→ Paper towel

→ Scissors

→ Small resealable plastic bag

→ Water

→ Uncooked dried beans, peas, or seeds

PLANT A BEAN IN A PLASTIC BAG AND WATCH ROOTS FORM AND LEAVES EMERGE BEFORE YOUR VERY EYES.

SAFETY
TIPS & HINTS

Dried beans are choking hazards for small children.

This experiment will work best with beans that are not too old and haven't been irradiated. You can soak them overnight before doing the experiment to make them sprout more quickly.

For this experiment, choose a window where the beans you plant get plenty of light, but won't be blasted by intense sun all day.

PROTOCOL

STEP 1: Cut a paper towel in half and fold it a few times so it will fit into the plastic ba

STEP 2: Soak the paper towel with water, squeeze out the excess, and put it into the bag. Smooth it so that it's relatively flat. (Fig. 1)

STEP 3: Plant two or three beans or seeds about 1 ¼ inches (3 cm) from the bottom the bag, on the same side of the paper towel. Don't worry if they don't stay in place, b if necessary, stuff a little piece of paper towel into the bottom of the bag so the seeds don't sit in water. (Fig. 2)

STEP 4: Seal the bag partway, but leave an opening near the top so the plants can g some air.

STEP 5: Tape the bag in a window with the beans facing you so you can watch them they grow. (Fig. 3, 4)

Fig. 1: Soak the paper towel in water.

Fig. 2: Plant two or three beans in your bag.

Fig. 3: Hang the bag in a window, with the beans facing in toward you.

Fig. 4: Soon your beans will start to sprout and grow.

THE SCIENCE
BEHIND THE FUN:

Seeds, such as dried beans and peas, contain dormant baby plants. Dormant literally means "sleeping." These tiny plants need certain signals to make them "wake up" and emerge from the seed. Germination is the name for the processes the embryonic plant goes through to sprout from the seed and form leaves.

Environmental signals that plants need to germinate include adequate light, air, and water. Temperature can also play a role in germination.

When a plant first sprouts, it gets the nutrients it needs from the seed. In this experiment, you can see the seed shrink as the plant grows. As a plant matures, it will depend on roots and leaves to collect the energy it needs. Once it reaches a certain size and completely uses up the nutrients in the seed, your window sprout will have to be transplanted to nutrient-rich soil to survive.

CREATIVE
ENRICHMENT

Record the beans' germination by drawing and measuring them each day. Record your data in a science notebook. What happens if you do the same experiment, but put one bag of beans in a window and another one in a dark closet?

SOLAR STILL SURVIVAL SCIENCE

MATERIALS

→ Large bowl

→ Small bowl, whose rim is lower than the rim of the big bowl

→ 1 cup (235 ml) tap water

→ A few tablespoons (40 g) salt

→ Food coloring

→ Plastic wrap

→ Marble or pebble

HARNESS THE SUN'S ENERGY TO PURIFY WATER.

Fig. 3: Put your solar still in the sun and wa for pure water to drip into the small bowl.

SAFETY TIPS & HINTS

This experiment works best on a hot, sunny day because it utilizes the sun's energy to clean the water.

STEP 1: Put the small bowl inside the big bowl.

STEP 2: Mix the tap water, salt, and a drop or two of food coloring. This is your "contaminated" water. (Fig. 1)

STEP 3: Pour the salt water into the big bowl, making sure the liquid stays outside of your small bowl, because you'll be collecting clean water in the small bowl.

STEP 4: Loosely cover the top of the large bowl with a single piece of plastic wrap. Place a marble or pebble in the center of the plastic wrap and adjust the wrap so that there is a slight dip directly above the small collection bowl. Seal the plastic wrap around the edges of the bowl as well as you can. (Fig. 2)

STEP 5: Place the bowl in the sunlight and observe it every few hours. Adjust plastic wrap as needed, so condensation drips into the small bowl. (Fig. 3)

Fig. 1: Add salt and food coloring to some water to "contaminate" it.

Fig. 2: Cover the large bowl with plastic wrap.

STEP 6: When you've collected enough purified water, which can take a day or two, you can taste the water to see how your purifier worked. Be sure to wipe the bottom of the collection bowl before you pour it out so you don't contaminate your clean water!

||| THE SCIENCE BEHIND THE FUN:

The sun's ultraviolet rays will travel through the plastic wrap and into the colored water, where they're absorbed and rereleased as heat energy. Because the heat can't escape back out through the plastic wrap, the air and water in the bowl heat up.

In your solar still, the warmer temperature helps water molecules on the surface evaporate into the air in the bowl, leaving the salt and food coloring behind in the big bowl. When they collide with the plastic wrap, the water molecules encounter a cooler surface, since the air outside the bowl is not as warm. The clean water then condenses, or forms droplets, on the plastic wrap. When the droplets get big enough, gravity pulls them to the lowest part of the plastic wrap and they drip into the collection container, leaving you with pure water.

CREATIVE ENRICHMENT

☀ Add vinegar to contaminate your water, purify it using a solar still, and check the pH of both your starting and purified water using litmus paper, which you can buy online or at large department store chains.

PIZZA BOX SOLAR OVEN

MATERIALS

→ Pizza box

→ Marker or pen

→ Ruler

→ Scissors

→ Aluminum foil

→ Tape

→ Black construction paper

→ Newspaper

→ Clear plastic wrap

→ Dowel or stick to prop the box lid up

→ Snack to warm in your oven (e.g., chocolate, marshmallows, cookies)

SAFETY TIPS & HINTS

This oven is intended for heating up snacks, such as chocolate and cookies, and should never be used to cook raw meat or anything that can spoil when warm.

Do this experiment on a sunny day.

Very young kids may need assistance cutting the box.

BUILD A SNACK OVEN FROM A PIZZA BOX.

Fig. 3: Your oven is ready to go, with insulation, a window and a reflector. This one needs one more roll of newspaper in the back.

PROTOCOL

STEP 1: Draw a square on the top of your pizza box, leaving a frame of at least 2 inches (5 cm) on each side of the square. Scribble out the line closest to the hinge on the box and cut along the other three lines to make a second hinged lid. (Fig. 1)

STEP 2: Gently fold the flap back along the uncut edge of the square to form a crease. The flap should fold back toward the hinge of the pizza box. Wrap the underside (inside) face of the flap that you made with aluminum foil. Secure the foil with tape outside the lid. This is your reflector.

STEP 3: Open the pizza box and cover the bottom of it with black construction paper.

STEP 4: Stack and tightly roll up several pieces of newspaper. Fit the newspaper rolls around the inside perimeter of the box as insulation. The rolls should be about 2 inches (5 cm) thick. Secure the insulation with tape to the bottom of the box. Be sure you can close the original lid on your pizza box.

STEP 5: Cut two pieces of plastic wrap about 2 inches (5 cm) larger than the hole you cut in the original pizza box top. Open the lid of your pizza box and tape one piece of plastic wrap to the underside of the hole in the pizza box lid. (Fig. 2)

STEP 6: Lift the reflector flap. Tape another piece of plastic wrap over the top of the hole in your pizza box lid. This pocket of plastic wrap is like a double-paned window and creates a layer of air as insulation to keep heat in the box. Make sure the plastic wrap is tight. (Fig. 3)

STEP 7: Take your oven outside, put it on a flat surface facing the sun, and put the food you want to cook inside, on the black paper. Close the lid tightly and open the foil reflecting flap so sunlight strikes the black paper and food in the oven. (Fig. 4)

STEP 8: Prop open the reflecting flap, using a dowel or stick or the ruler. Play with the angle of the flap to see how much sunlight you can get to reflect from the foil lid directly onto the food in the oven.

STEP 9: Wait for your oven to heat up. Check every 5 minutes to see how well your food is being heated by solar thermal energy. When it's done, enjoy your snack. (Fig. 5)

Fig. 1: Cut three sides of a square into the lid of your box to create a hinged lid.

Fig. 2: Tape plastic wrap on both sides of the hole on your pizza box lid.

Fig. 4: Position your oven in the sun, with the foil reflecting light into the box.

Fig. 5: Enjoy your snack.

THE SCIENCE
BEHIND THE FUN:

The sun's rays travel through the double layers of plastic wrap and are absorbed by the black paper at the bottom of your oven, where they're converted to heat energy. This new form of energy can't escape the plastic wrap and the newspaper insulation you added helps keep the heat energy captive in the oven.

The aluminum foil reflector you made directs additional ultraviolet rays into your oven, adding more energy to the mix. As your solar oven sits in the sun, more and more energy enters the pizza box, but most of it can't escape. The increasing heat energy drives up the temperature inside your oven, making it hot enough to warm your snack.

CREATIVE ENRICHMENT

Use a thermometer to monitor the oven temperature. How warm will your oven get on a sunny day versus on a cloudy day? Does the air temperature outside the oven have an effect on oven temperature?

Ava
 Cooper
John
Cece
 Georgia
Croix
 Reagan
 Jace

May
Henri
 Charlie
 Claire
AJ
 Nicholas
Kate
 Bristow

 Scarlett
Cela
Lila
Liz
Ava
Natalie
 Miriam
Lauren

 Sarah
 Geneva
 Lily
 Ella
Hailey
 Enzo
 Claire
 Whitney

 Nick
 Elena
 Nico
 Lyuda
 Catherine
 Stella
Mia
 Alessa

Emmett
Nate
Theo
Will
 Sienna
 Corah
 Ayla
 Norah

 Sarah
Mark
 Charlie
 Andrew
 Carissa
 Kyra
 Harper
 Ian

RESOURCES

CHEMISTRY
acswebcontent.acs.org/scienceforkids/index.html

MICROBIOLOGY
sciencebuddies.org/science-fair-projects/project_ideas/
MicroBio_Interpreting_Plates.shtml

CLIMATE
climate.nasa.gov
climatekids.nasa.gov

ROCKET SCIENCE
jpl.nasa.gov/education/students
nasa.gov/audience/forkids/kidsclub/flash/#.Unj_fvmsi-0

WATER
education.usgs.gov
ga.water.usgs.gov/edu/watercycle-kids-adv.html

LIGHT AND COLOR
education.web.cern.ch/education/Chapter2/Intro.html

RENEWABLE ENERGY
nrel.gov/science_technology

CRYSTALS
smithsonianeducation.org/educators/lesson_plans/
minerals/minerals_crystals.html

SOLAR SCIENCE
solarscience.msfc.nasa.gov

ALL THINGS SPACE AND EARTH SCIENCE
nasa.gov

ABOUT THE AUTHOR

Liz Heinecke has loved science since she was old enough to inspect her first butterfly.

After working in molecular biology research for ten years and getting her master's degree, she left the lab to kick off a new chapter in her life as a stay-at-home mom. Soon she found herself sharing her love of science with her three kids as they grew, journaling their science adventures on her KitchenPantryScientist website.

Her desire to spread her enthusiasm for science to others soon led to a regular segment on her local NBC affiliate, an opportunity to serve as an Earth Ambassador for NASA, and the creation of an iPhone app, with the goal of making it simple for parents to do science with kids of all ages, and for kids to experiment safely on their own.

You can find her at home in Minnesota, wrangling her kids, writing for her website, updating the KidScience app, teaching microbiology to nursing students, singing, playing banjo, painting, running, and doing almost anything else to avoid housework.

Liz graduated from Luther College and received her master's degree in bacteriology from the University of Wisconsin, Madison.

GLOSSARY

Acid—a chemical that forms hydrogen ions when dissolved in water and combines with bases in a chemical reaction

Acid-base indicator—a substance that determines the acidity or basicity of a solution by changing color

Atom—the smallest unit of a chemical element

Atomic bond—a chemical bond that occurs through the transfer of or sharing of electrons between atoms

Bacterial growth media—a combination of nutrients and chemicals used to grow different types of cells

Base—a substance that accepts hydrogen ions when dissolved in water and combines with acids in a chemical reaction

Capillary action—the main force that allows the movement of water up into plants

Centrifuge—a machine that spins very fast to separate objects or cells by separating their dense center

Colony (microbial)—a cluster of microorganisms grown from a single cell on a medium

Crystal—solids formed by a network of repeating patterns of molecules connected by atomic bonds

Density—mass (how many atoms are in an object) divided by volume (how much space an object takes up)

Dermatoglyphics—the scientific study of fingerprints

Drag—a force that acts opposite to the way an object is moving

Element—a substance that cannot be broken down into simple substances by ordinary chemical means

Epidermis—the outer layer of skin

Force—something that causes a change in an object's motion (mass multiplied by acceleration)

Fragment—a small piece of a whole

Freezing point—the temperature at which a liquid turns into a solid

Friction—resistance that occurs when one object rubs against another

Fungi (plural of fungus)—eukaryotic organisms that live and grow by decomposing organic material around them

Gas—one of the three states of matter that can expand freely to take up any available space

Gradient—the separation of areas that contain a high and low number of particles

Gravity—an attracting force between two objects with mass, such as Earth's gravity, which attracts objects to the center of the earth

Inertia—objects do not want to change the speed to which they're moving or not moving, the heavier the object is, the more inertia it has

Liquid—one of the three states of matter that flows freely and takes the shape of its container

Mass—how many atoms are in an object

Membrane—the protective outer layer of a cell

Microbe—a form of life that can only be seen with a microscope, including the fungi and bacteria that live on your body and every surface you see around you

Molecule—the smallest amount of a specific chemical substance that can exist alone

Nucleic acid—acids that make up the genetic material of all cells, DNA or RNA

Pigment—molecules that give things color

Pressure—the force on a given area or how much one thing is pushing on something else

Prism—a triangular object made of glass or quartz that can separate white light into colors

Solid—one of the three states of matter that has a definite shape

Starch—an organic chemical that is produced by all green plants

Supersaturated solution—a solution that is forced to hold more atoms in water (or another solute) than it normally would

Surface tension—a force on a layer of liquid that causes it to act like an elastic skin and hold the liquid together, for example, it allows small insects to walk on water

Transpiration—the release of water absorbed by plant roots, by tiny pores on called stromata on the underside of leaves, which helps water overcome the force of and reach the leaves in very tall trees

Common Kitchen Chemicals

Acetic acid—vinegar

Glucose syrup—corn syrup

Glucose-fructose syrup—high fructose corn syrup

Sodium bicarbonate—baking soda

Sodium chloride—table salt

Sucrose—table sugar

INDEX